RICO PETROCELLI

BOSTON RED SOX HALL OF FAMER

"Kevin has written a terrific book that will improve the hitting skills of boys and girls of all ages. Parents, Little League coaches, as well as, College and High School coaches can help their players become much better hitters by using the technique that Kevin explains in this book.

Top Hand Hitting will help the athlete make more contact and still be able to hit the ball out of the park. This is a must read for anyone who wants to teach hitting skills. Kevin knows it works by his experience playing and his extensive research on the subject. This method helped me hit 40 home runs one year in the major leagues."

RICO PETROCELLI

www.ricopetrocelli.com

PRAISE FOR "TEACH YOUR KID TO HIT..."

JEFF FRYE

**MAJOR LEAGUE BASEBALL STAR,
OWNER OF THE VIRAL WEBSITE WWW.SHEGONEHITTING.COM**

"My friend Kevin Gallagher's book "Teach Your Kid to Hit...So They Don't Quit" is perfect for parents who want to teach their kids the fundamentals of hitting. There are many self-proclaimed "hitting gurus" out there teaching kids the wrong way to hit that will result in failure, and eventually kids will quit playing. This book covers the basics that all kids need to learn to be successful baseball or softball hitters.

The fundamentals in this book are fundamentals for a reason. They are the same fundamentals I learned and used during my 15-year professional baseball career. These fundamentals helped me hit .290 as a Major Leaguer for the Rangers, Red Sox, Rockies and Blue Jays."

JEFF FRYE

www.shegonehitting.com

BASEBALL

Teach Your Kid to Hit

...SO THEY DON'T QUIT!

Parents—YOU Can Teach Them, Promise!

KEVIN GALLAGHER

ILLUSTRATED BY CEEJ ROWLAND

Foreword by Rick Wolff

Endorsed by **RICO PETROCELLI**

KG | PUBLISHING

ESTERO, FLORIDA

Baseball: Teach Your Kid to Hit...So They Don't Quit
Parents—YOU Can Teach Them, Promise!

1st Edition 2020, 2nd Edition 2021

ISBN: 978-1-7347271-1-1 Paperback, full color images

ISBN: 978-1-7347271-4-2 Paperback, black and white images

ISBN: 978-1-7347271-5-9 eBook, full color images

Printed in the United States of America

Illustrations by Ceej Rowland

Book Formatting and Cover Design by Becky's Graphic Design®, LLC

BeckysGraphicDesign.com

FOREWORD

When I was growing up and, like so many other little kids of my generation who loved baseball and who loved to hit, I can recall reading Ted Williams' classic book, THE SCIENCE OF HITTING.

Even to this day, decades later, I can still remember reading about the Hall of Famer's approach to hitting. For Ted, the absolute best way to hit was to lower one' back shoulder and then swing at the incoming pitch with a solid and powerful upper-cut swing.

This was the way hitting was taught to kids everywhere. After all, who would ever challenge the wisdom of one of the game's greatest hitters? But bear in mind that Ted was a left-handed hitter with great power, and he stood 6'4" with 20/10 pinpoint vision.

Fast forward from when I was a little kid to when I was a senior in high school. Not to be immodest, but I set all sorts of batting records at Edgemont High School. I attributed my success to the batting instruction from what I memorized from Ted's bestselling book. Clearly his advice was working for me, and doing so in a big and very satisfying way.

For myself, a 6-0 right-handed hitting infielder, I was blessed with excellent eyesight. I also had a little power, although in truth, nothing like Ted Williams.

Photo Credit: Detroit Tigers

I graduated from Edgemont, and then made the jump to Division I baseball with great expectations. But suddenly everything changed. I maintained my Ted Williams-styled upper cut swing with my back shoulder dropping down, but in college, it was no longer working.

The simple answer? The velocity of the pitches I was seeing in college was dramatically faster than what I saw in high school, and as a result, I couldn't swing my bat fast enough. I was getting jammed and breaking bats all the time. When I tried to overcompensate and swing the bat sooner, I just ended up being easily fooled by curves and change-ups.

It was bleak. And frustrating.

Then, in the summer between my freshman and sophomore year, I got a big break. I played for a wonderful coach named Al Goldis, in the Atlantic Collegiate Baseball League (ACBL). Al took one look at my swing, and said to me, "Rick, that upper cut swing may have worked for you in high school, but if you have any hopes of hitting well in college or even in the pro ranks, you're going to have to ditch that hitting style, and learn how to chop wood when you hit."

"Chop wood?" I asked.

Al laughed. "You have to learn how to use a Top-Hand Hitting approach. That's the only way you'll ever get the bat barrel fast enough into the hitting zone."

It was the best hitting advice I ever received. It didn't come easy, because I had to, in effect, re-program my entire life-long approach to hitting. But eventually I mastered enough of the top-hand approach to become an All-Star in the ACBL, was drafted by the Detroit Tigers and played a couple of years in their minor league system. I even recall in my first year of pro ball, I was the first player on my team to hit a home run that season. Not too bad for a kid who, just three years earlier, couldn't get around on a fastball.

The bottom line? A couple of important reminders: As a parent of a youth baseball player, first you need to know that hitting a baseball is very, very difficult. And that it's difficult for everyone. There are no exceptions.

The good news is that you have in your hands Kevin Gallagher's superb and insightful guide — "Teach Your Kid To Hit...So They Don't Quit!" on how to teach your child the right way to hit a baseball.

Kevin does a terrific job in outlining how any Mom or Dad can teach their youngster the basic – and right – approach to learning how to hit for the first time, or any time in their playing days when they begin to struggle.

His Top-Hand Hitting Process is straightforward and right to the point.

It was this exact Top Hand Hitting "best-advice" that I received later in my own playing days that turned my career around, and propelled me into Professional Baseball.

I only wish I had Kevin's book available to me when I was a kid!

All you need to add into the mix is patience and encouragement.

RICK WOLFF

SPRING 2020

Rick Wolff is one of the nation's leading experts on sports psychology, and also is the host of WFAN Sports Radio's "Rick Wolff's Sports Edge", the longest-running sports parenting radio show in the country. Find him at www.askcoachwolff.com.

SAVE THE GAME

I am releasing the 2ⁿᵈ edition of "Teach Your Kid to Hit...So They Don't Quit" to include some of the noteworthy endorsements "Teach" has received from Pro Ballplayers, Coaches, Journalists and ordinary fans over the past year.

Since the book went on sale in June of 2020, I have been asked to be a guest on dozens of TV, Podcast and Radio programs and have been featured in numerous Major Print publications all across the United States.

The response has been overwhelmingly positive as readers have embraced my 8 Step Top Hand Hitting Instruction in the book as being instrumental for parents and coaches to understand a simple process designed to teach their child to make contact with a baseball.

So many of the reactions across the country from baseball fans have also included the disillusionment of how hitting is taught today, emphasizing the "Lift Swing" or the 30° "Launch Angle" that has so negatively affected the success of their child and reduced the level of action and the "Entertainment" component of Major League Baseball.

This book, and the Top Hand Contact Hitting Process which I wrote two years ago was and is designed to help change the experience kids have playing the game, and to increase the enjoyment of fans watching it at all levels.

I encourage you to stay tuned as there is more to come from this Book, this Author, and a select group of influential baseball people and ordinary fans as we work with MLB and Amateur Leagues to provide a comprehensive solution to the entertainment and participation challenges baseball—our game—is facing today.

TOGETHER, WE CAN SAVE THE GAME!

If you are interested in changing the game, let me know!
EMAIL: baseballkgllg@gmail.com
WEBSITE: www.hittingsimple.com
FACEBOOK: Teach Your Kid to Hit

Kevin Gallagher, July 2021

"TEACH YOUR KID TO HIT...SO THEY DON'T QUIT"
ENDORSEMENTS

MEDIA APPEARANCES:

- *WFAN Radio NYC "The Sports Edge" with Rick Wolff – the longest running sports-parenting show in America. 23 years. Appeared in 2020 and in 2021.*

- *MLB Radio Network and Sirius XM with Rico Petrocelli and Ed Randall*

- *MLB TV Network and Perfect Game TV with Daron Sutton*

- *Numerous magazines, radio shows, TV, Podcasts across the U.S.*

COLLABORATION:

- *Boston Red Sox RBI Foundation using on website as their Instructional Tool... and working with Nike—their biggest Sponsor—to get books out to coaches in N.E.*

- *Little League International selling and promoting book to parents and coaches*

- *Baseball Hall of Fame Cooperstown NY Bookstore*

- **Perfect Game**, the largest Amateur Baseball Organization in America has the book on their website as "The Hitting Instructional Tool"

- **Dixie Boys Baseball** a 14 State League using the book as a "Hitting Tool" on all 14 state websites

- For sale on Jeff Frye's **www.shegonehitting.com** as a hitting instruction tool

- *Amazon #1 Hot New Release July 2020*

ENDORSEMENTS:

TOM WERNER – Chairman of the Boston Red Sox and the RBI Foundation

Selling the book as a tool for parents on the Red Sox RBI Foundation website (Revive Baseball in Inner Cities)

RICO PETROCELLI – Boston Red Sox Hall of Famer

"Kevin has written a terrific book, *Teach Your Kid to Hit...So They Don't Quit,* that will improve the hitting skills of boys and girls of all ages. Parents, Little League coaches, as well as, College and High School coaches can help their players become much better hitters by using the technique that Kevin explains in this book.

Top hand hitting will help the athlete make more contact and still be able to hit the ball out of the park. **This is a must read for anyone who wants to teach hitting skills.** Kevin knows it works by his experience playing and his extensive research on the subject. This method helped me hit 40 home runs one year in the major leagues."

KEVIN KERNAN – Sportswriter Hall of Famer and Author of Ballnine.com

"Listen to Kevin Gallagher who wrote a new fun how-to book called *Teach Your Kid to Hit...So They Don't Quit.*"

"The main thing is to get the barrel of the bat on the same plane as the ball for as quickly as you can, for as long as you can to create multiple points of contact for the kid to hit the ball."

That is a simple but brilliant point and a lot of major league hitters would do well to follow that advice.

This is a kids' book intended for parents, regardless of their baseball expertise. 118 pages and easy read.

The book has an eight-step process, and illustrations showing "Riley Dude" working the process. There are two-minute videos links included in the book for each Step, as well as on YouTube that work in conjunction with the easy to follow written instructions and illustrations."

Featured articles found here:

> https://ballnine.com/2020/12/27/stay-hitting-my-friends
> https://ballnine.com/2021/05/08/launch-this

RICK WOLFF – Former Professional Ballplayer and Host of WFAN Radio's "The Sports Edge"- the longest running Sports Parenting show in U.S. (23 years)

> "Kevin does a terrific job in his book *Teach Your Kid to Hit...So They Don't Quit*, outlining how any Mom or Dad can teach their youngster the basic – and right – approach to learning how to hit for the first time, or any time in their playing days when they begin to struggle. His Top-Hand Hitting Process is straightforward. I only wish I had Kevin's book available to me when I was a kid!"

ED RANDALL – Host "Remember When" on MLB Network Radio and "Ed Randall's Talking Baseball" on WFAN-Radio

> *Teach Your Kid to Hit...* is TERRIFIC, it's WONDERFUL. I wish I had this book when I was a kid."

JERRY FORD – Founder and President "Perfect Game" – largest amateur baseball organization in the U.S.

> "Kevin, your book *Teach Your Kid to Hit... So They Don't Quit* and more important your reason for writing it is very interesting. I can't imagine why we wouldn't endorse it.

> As Founder and President of Perfect Game, an Organization created to promote the game of baseball now and in the future, I highly recommend *Teach Your Kid to Hit...So They Don't Quit* by Kevin Gallagher.

> For any parent that wants to "teach" their kid to make contact with the

ball – this is the book. Kevin's approach is to ensure that any parent has a simple but effective tool to teach their child to hit, have fun and stay with the game of baseball.

This book is a fun but insightful read highlighting what "doesn't work", mistakes parents and coaches make and in conclusion offers the solution in an 8 Step Top Hand Hitting Instruction delivered in written and illustrative form, accompanied by a 2 minute video for each step.

If a child isn't hitting the ball, they will quit the game. ***Teach Your Kid...*** will empower you to ensure your child makes contact with the ball, has fun and will allow both of you to create memories on the ballfield for years to come!

Kevin has the qualifications and experience to help many young kids stay involved in the game of baseball.

I for one, think this book will help many people.

SANDY JONES – Commissioner Dixie Boys Baseball, 14 State Baseball League

"Kevin's instruction for Parents has uniqueness. I do think that the concepts found in your book are very sound and would prove to be very helpful. It is very important that youth receive instruction on how to hit and we must improve our success rate if our goal is to keep kids playing the game"

HENRY MANNING – Pace University Head Coach, AAA Player with the Chicago White Sox

"Kevin, in his new book ***Teach Your Kid to Hit... So They Don't Quit*** does a great job of explaining the swing so kids and parents can understand it without being overwhelmed. With so many other options out there for kids, the book is written in a way to make the game fun and to keep kids playing baseball."

DAVID POPOWICH – Major League Employee (MLB), Coach, Dad, Lifelong baseball player and Fan

"...after reading the opening to the book I felt that Kevin was talking directly to me. I lived the struggle with a 12-year-old son having trouble making contact when batting.

After completing the book and online videos, we got to work. Two weeks of work, and then during the next USSSA Tournament my son made more contact, collected a few hits and wanted more!

The book helped tremendously.... And we continue to work the process!"

Review from a READER ON INGRAM SPARK (Barnes & Noble)

"I'm an assistant coach for my son's 6U tee ball team as well as an assistant for our town's All Star travel team in Florida. My son is an above average athlete but having taught the methods outlined in this book to him, he became a monster hitter leading his recreational team to 1st place and currently is the best hitter on his All Star travel team.

Before I read the book, ***Teach Your Kid to Hit... So They Don't Quit***, my son had a golf swing, which when he made contact would go far but the consistency was nowhere to be found. With Kevin's top hand approach, my son's swing has become incredibly consistent and is making solid powerful contact each and every time he's at bat. My son went 7 for 8 yesterday with 5 home runs, triple and a single and these hits were all hard line drives with height that reached the fence… Simply amazing.

Needless to say, I have been teaching the top hand approach to our team since September and the results have been incredible. Do keep in mind this is not an overnight process. The method needs to be reinforced constantly and you must put the time in with your child/team with tee work and batting practice. My players' parents are forever grateful for what I have been able to teach their kids and they're constantly asking me to be their kids' hitting coach going forward.

This book is a must for any coach that wants to teach proper hitting."

RENE DELAVARRE – Winner of the Teach Your Kid endorsement contest and former South Carolina University Baseball Standout

"Parents who love baseball and want their son/daughter to be great must read this book.

Written by a student of baseball, Kevin Gallagher has written a gem of book. You will not get this information from any Little League or high school coach!

This book will prevent your budding ballplayer from "swinging thru air."

The key: keeping the bat on an even plane as the ball approaches the hitter.

This book teaches this technique. If I had had this information available to me when I was playing in high school and college, perhaps I might have made it to the pros."

VIC ORTIZ – Winner of the Teach Your Kid endorsement contest and former ABC News Producer and Director

A delightful and must read for all baseball enthusiasts.

"In his new book "Teach Your Kid to Hit...So They Don't Quit!' Kevin uses a no-nonsense approach, with detailed illustrations and concise coaching in which your child, no matter his or her skill levels, will learn how to improve their fundamentals and gain keen insight into the finer points of hitting

If you are a parent or grandparent and love baseball or coach baseball... you should have this book and share this information with all the people you can. Kevin's book is a must read for all baseball fans."

Table of Contents

STOP
READ THIS FIRST!

Most people skip over anything before Chapter One, but I wanted to get your attention to ensure you read this short entry before reading Chapter One and before starting the book.

When you read this section, you will realize that this is not just an Instructional Book, but a story as to why this book was written and how to get the most out of it...So you as a parent or coach can own the ideas, philosophy, and process and be able to pass it along as "YOURS."

This story will tell you about the state of baseball today, how people complicate teaching the art of hitting a baseball, why parents struggle to get their kids to hit, and why kids get frustrated and quit the game.

We will discuss and compare the "Solution" of Top Hand Hitting throughout.

And by the time you get to the 8 Step Instructional process (written and video) at the end of the book, you will understand the approach, the reason why it will work and you will believe in it.

Oh...It is so important that you believe in it!

And you will.

To start off with, I want you to understand that the text of this book is intended for **parents** to read, not the child, so they can learn a process to teach their child how to hit a baseball or softball, and make consistent contact.

And also, that this book is intended for **parents to teach both boys and girls** as the method and process applies equally to both, whether they are playing Baseball or Softball.

For ease and flow of reading, I may refer to "him" or "he" more often than "her" or "she", but make no mistake this is written for the **"both"**.

The text of the book, the stories, statistics, and anecdotes are intended for the **parents** to read and understand, while the videos are intended for the **parents** to absorb and use to teach the child.

But I have also included dozens of **Illustrations for the child** and created a unique character named **"Riley Dude"** to help the child learn. He appears in all the illustrations throughout the book wherever a visual aid is needed.

When you, as a parent may be having difficulty conveying something to your child, you can show him how **"Riley Dude"** is doing it.

"Riley Dude" and the Illustrations, are colorful and entertaining and are intended for the **child** to look at, so they can understand what the main character is doing, which can help you convey the process to them.

"Riley Dude" and the Illustrations are another tool for the parent to use to explain to your child what you are teaching, and why.

Visual understanding is extremely important for the viewer to understand what is being taught and more importantly, why. That is why I have included many Illustrations for the child to enjoy while also learning from them, and an 8 Step Video Process for the Parent.

People don't learn and retain things because they are told something, but rather because they are involved in the process, then understand it and eventually own it.

There is a saying that I have found to be very accurate...

"Tell me something and I will forget it. Show me something and I may remember it. But involve me in the process, ahhhh...then I will understand it. And when I understand it, I own it. And when I own it, I can take it with me where ever I go".

Many readers may want to skip to the end of this book to get to the 8 Step Process. I urge you to read the entire book before you get to the Steps so you understand the WHAT and the WHY.

You should find this book entertaining as well as informative.

When you read the entire book:

- You will become **involved** in the process.

- You will **understand** why it is important

- You will **understand** the drawbacks of certain methods being taught today.

- You will **believe** in the style and process and you will **own** it. It will become yours!

- You will then have a method, a style, a process that becomes **"you"** and you can take it with you wherever you go.

- You will have the **confidence** to not only teach it to children, but also **believe** in it, and then explain it to others. It will become a **"part"** of who you are.

- You will have the opportunity to **change peoples' lives**. Children and adults.

Just as a reminder—you will find I repeat certain points throughout the book. It is not by mistake, but rather for **emphasis.**

THE DAVE F. STORY

7 WORDS. 7 VERY POWERFUL WORDS

Who is Dave F. and why I am writing about him?

Dave F. is a unique and caring individual but in the context of this subject, Dave F. is more than one person. He represents millions of kids. He wanted to play the game of baseball but didn't know how to hit. Most kids aren't born knowing how to hit. They need to be taught.

Parents and volunteers do the best they can, and encourage, help and give of their time but many lack the know how to teach a kid to make contact.

The first of many powerful reactions I received from readers shortly after I released this book was from Dave F. As mentioned, Dave wanted desperately to play baseball and learn to hit. Unfortunately, the coaches he had lacked the tools to teach him.

They assembled the kids, threw Batting Practice and took mental notes that went like this ... "Billy can hit, Tom can't, Joey can, Dave can't..." and from there they picked their team and created their lineup.

Sound familiar?

Those that struggled to make contact were either cut or classified into that "other" category that sat at the end of the bench or maybe didn't get into the game. They essentially became invisible. This silent classification can have a huge impact on a child's social and emotional development.

What Dave F. wrote to me right after the book was released and he read it was profound. It was only 7 words, but 7 very powerful and poignant words.

He wrote... "Thank you Kevin. I AM that kid."

This was from a 64-year-old man who didn't say he "WAS" that kid – he said I "AM" that kid.

He remembers vividly the feelings of embarrassment and rejection that helped shape his self-esteem. It affected who is his friends became, what social circles he traveled in, the parties he was invited to, his confidence to take risks in the future... his feeling left out, separate.

All this from 55 years ago. Still clear and imbedded in his psyche.

Dave stopped playing baseball.

This book aims to change that for kids today.

"Teach Your Kid to Hit...So They Don't Quit"

CHAPTER 1
Purpose of the Book

The purpose of this book is two-fold:

1. To teach young children how to hit a baseball so they can have fun.

2. To help parents realize that **they** are the ones who can teach their child how to hit and have fun.

What I am not trying to do is:

- I am **NOT** trying to create a singular, universal way of hitting designed to turn your child into a prodigy.

- I am **NOT** trying to create an "Academy" for major league prospects or college scholarship athletes (although the method I will describe can be used for all levels of talent, even those with exceptional talent).

- I will **NOT** be talking about Torque, or Rotating the hips or any other complicated jargon that will only confuse your child, and is unnecessary.

Rather, what this book is meant to do is:

To provide a process to teach **ordinary kids**, who like, and want to play baseball, how to make contact with a pitched ball so they don't get frustrated and quit.

- I am endeavoring to teach them a way to hit the ball more often and consequently have fun.

- When children have fun, they will want to continue to have fun...but when something is too difficult, it creates frustration and eventually embarrassment, and children will look to something else to have fun.

- They will leave the game of baseball.

AND...to convince parents that **THEY** are the ones that can learn this process, and teach their child to hit.

- Most parents don't know how to teach their child to hit...As a matter of fact, most Little League and many High School coaches don't know how to teach a child to hit.

- Parents will devote time and throw Batting Practice (BP) and encourage their child, but don't have a process or a specific set of instructions that will **MAKE SENSE** to the child or that will work for their child.

Kids will lose interest quickly if they fail and will leave the game.

It doesn't matter how much **you** love the game, **they** will leave.

It is our responsibility to teach them and keep them!

So remember, we need to **"Teach Your Kid To Hit...So They Don't Quit"**

CHAPTER 2
Process to Success

Success is usually the result of a plan, a process. It is a culmination of thought, planning, and then action.

Success rarely happens by accident.

What we will discuss in this book is a plan, a process or a set of instructions to teach anyone how to make contact with a baseball.

I always find it helpful when a speaker summarizes ahead of time what they will be speaking about, so I don't have to discover it along the way.

As a matter of fact, I like it when before they start they tell me what they are going to speak about, speak about it, and then summarize what they just spoke about. The subject matter usually sticks better that way.

So before we begin, let me tell you what we will be discussing in the book, then I will tell you, and at the end summarize it for emphasis.

This book and the process will focus on the following points:

- A set of instructions that make sense to you **and** your child.

- It will involve **Contact Hitting** using a **Level Swing**.

- It will utilize **Top Hand Hitting**, stressing a dominant **Top Hand** at all times.

- It will stress getting the **Barrel of the Bat** from its Starting Point to the **Contact Point** using the shortest distance (straight line).

- We will get the **Barrel of the Bat** on the **same plane that the ball is traveling, as quickly as we can and for as long as we can**, to create multiple contact points for the bat to hit the ball (or the ball to hit the bat.)

What we will layout is a blueprint for **you as a parent** to provide to your child, that will produce success, and a blueprint to go back to if your child encounters difficulty later on due to sloppy habits, or when the competition speeds up as he progresses in ranks.

A STYLE OF HITTING THAT ISN'T JUST FOR KIDS STARTING OUT

So, I have written a book to teach kids, just starting out, how to make contact with a baseball.

But make no mistake about it, it is a method that will work for anyone at any age and any level. Personally, I used this method, with much success, throughout my career up and until I got injured in a Spring Training game with the Class A Pittsburgh Pirates in Bradenton.

Contact hitting, in the age of Home Run hitting, is beginning to make a comeback as people realize the importance of putting the ball in play, particularly in contact necessary situations.

Children and young adults can have success sometimes, using any style of hitting they want, given they have certain athletic and hand-eye coordination abilities. But one day, for most people, the natural style they use may stop working when the competition levels surpass their style.

Everyone eventually walks away from the game when they are no longer successful. When the competition exceeds their talent. They either get cut, or simply don't make the team at the next level, or leave due to frustration of not succeeding.

Every level we move up to narrows the number of people involved, and thus the talent pool gets smaller and better and only the topflight players continue.

Some leave when going from Little League to Babe Ruth, or into High School, or JV to Varsity...or to college.

Some never start because it is too hard for them from the beginning.

For many, their departure time may be premature. The style of hitting they always used stops working as the game speeds up, but what if they changed their style of hitting at that point? Would they find new success using a Contact or **Top Hand Hitting** style?

Could they continue for another period of time extending their playing days?

I believe so.

Contact Hitting and Top Hand Hitting could do for those athletes, later in their playing days, what it can do for kids starting out. Make contact. Find success. Have fun. Keep playing!

CHAPTER 3
Swinging and Missing...Good?

Have you ever heard this type of commentary from announcers?

"Swing and a miss. Strike 3! He swung right through that fastball Bob."

"Yes he did Tom. If he ever made contact with that swing, the ball would have gone a mile...what a beautiful swing."

Wait a minute. What? You can't swing through a baseball. That's impossible. And they are praising him for striking out...just because the batter looked good doing it?

The photo on the previous page is a New York Yankee player, using an "Upper Cut or Launch Angle Swing" it looks as though he "swung right through that ball". It is a beautiful swing. But he swung and missed.

As I will explain, this is because the Barrel of the Bat in the Launch Angle Swing always travels underneath the trajectory of the ball.

*This happens because the **Top Hand** becomes the Bottom Hand, the Barrel of the Bat always follows the **Top Hand**, and then the Barrel must come back up creating only ONE SINGULAR SPOT to make contact - difficult and needs perfect timing. ©ZUMA Press/ZUMA Press*

Swinging and missing in baseball has become an epidemic. And it is accepted as the norm now.

The shame or anger that used to accompany swinging and missing and striking out, isn't as present anymore in the Big Leagues or the ladder leagues to pro ball. The swing and miss is considered part of the price to pay for when you do make contact and hit the ball a long way.

This isn't right, and it wasn't always this way. The way hitting is taught today in many circles, it emphasizes an uppercut swing, or a launch angle, that when successful, produces long fly balls or home runs. But it also produces a lot of swings and misses.

But our kids, if taught this way, or no way at all, will not take striking out in stride. They will grow tired of the frustration and embarrassment of swinging and missing, and may leave the game of baseball way before they should. This is a major, if not the main reason, for the declining popularity amongst the youth in America.

I am writing this book to shine a light on another way to teach hitting...**Contact Hitting. Top Hand Hitting.**

*In this photo you can see the batters **Top Hand** has directed the Barrel of the Bat onto the same path of the ball throughout his swing, creating a Level Swing and multiple points of contact along the path of the ball. The **Top Hand** ALWAYS remains on top. ©ZUMA Press/ZUMA Press*

This is a method that can be used at every level of baseball, from the backyard to Little League, through High School and College, and into Professional Baseball.

But in starting out it is a method that will keep youngsters involved and enjoying baseball by producing results that are successful.

The basic premise of Contact Hitting/ **Top Hand Hitting** is **to get the bat on the same path that the ball is traveling as quickly as possible and keep it there as long as possible.**

This will increase the odds and frequency of hitting the ball or in many cases, the "ball hitting the bat."

Hitting a baseball is difficult and if children don't find some level of success early, children will be discouraged and move on to other types of activities.

Even YOUR child.

Baseball in America is losing popularity at the Major League level and this filters down to our youth. Children are choosing other options when it comes to sports.

The reasons for this are varied but one of the biggest ones is that hitting a baseball is hard.

Without proper instruction, and some level of success, children will find other interests to pursue.

We need to provide them with a process or method to hitting that makes sense to them...and will provide positive results.

I have a method that will allow normal parents to teach their kids how to hit a baseball. A step by step process that is simple. Most good things are.

If kids can find success, have fun and avoid the embarrassing swing and miss, over and over, we can keep youngsters in the game of baseball longer...from kids just starting out in Little League up through Babe Ruth and on into High School...and beyond.

The approach I am suggesting here will help anyone at any level to make more contact with the baseball

This book however, is especially good for the kids just starting out and for the parents who want to teach them the game they love but lack the know-how.

It will lay out a simple concept and approach to hitting a baseball.

I want to convince parents that they can teach their child to make contact with the baseball.

Yes, Mom and Dad, YOU can teach your child to hit!

CHAPTER 4

The State of Baseball Today

Before we get into the method of teaching contact hitting and inspiring children to continue playing baseball, let's take a look at why it is important.

- The game of baseball, once the undisputed National Pastime, has been relegated to a second-class citizen to the NFL. It has lost viewership and lost the interest and involvement of both adults as well as the youth of this country.

- America wants to see more scoring and more action as Baseball competes against Football and Basketball, two sports that have a faster pace and more excitement.

- But the constant swinging and missing based on the latest trend of teaching hitting which leans towards power, creates less action.

- We see the game at the professional level having a much larger Hispanic population, and a burgeoning Asian influence, exceptional athletes for sure, but both segments from outside the U.S.

- In 2017 the percentage of foreign-born players, mainly Hispanic as well as from Asian markets in MLB was 29.8%.

- We also see a much smaller involvement of youth from the African American population.

- In 1981, 18.7% of MLB players were African American. In 2019, however, only 7.7% of MLB players are African American. Put another way, 68 out of 882 MLB players are African American.

Our kids here in America have lost interest in the National Pastime, as well as a lot of Adults too.

Did you know that in 2019 the per-game attendance dropped to its lowest point in 16 years?

The reasons for this are varied but certainly focus on the fact that:

GAMES ARE TAKING TOO LONG.

- In 1920 the average time for an MLB game was 1hr and 51 minutes
- In the 1970's the average length was 2 hours and 30 minutes.
- In 2017 the average time for a game was 3 hours and 5 minutes.
- So, in 2017 there were many games approaching 3½ to 4 hours. Given that baseball is played virtually every day for 6 months very few people, including kids, have the time or attention span to watch complete games on a regular basis taking as long as they do.

TELEVISED GAMES END TOO LATE AND LOSE YOUTH VIEWERSHIP

- In the 1960s and 1970s games started later and ended earlier.
- Typically, games were shorter and ended by 10 pm giving kids a shot at watching an entire game.
- Today they start earlier but still end later.
- Games ending in local markets past 11 pm is not uncommon.

THERE IS LESS ACTION INSIDE EACH GAME

- In 2018 the time between balls put in play (batter contact) was 3 minutes and 40 seconds. 3 minutes and 40 seconds! That is a lot of standing around for a casual viewer to watch.

- And did you realize that in 2018 over 1/3 (34%) of all plate appearances in MLB resulted in either a Walk, Strikeout, or a Home Run?

- This means that over 1/3 of each game involves only 2 defensive players... the pitcher and catcher? Everyone else stands around...BORING to play and BORING to watch!

Or as Pete Rose recently said, "Home Runs are up, strikeouts are up, and attendance is down. I didn't go to Harvard, but this is not a good thing."

These are issues that MLB must address. So why bring them up here where we are talking about kids in Little League?

I bring them up here because if kids are less interested in the game itself, attend fewer games and watch it less on TV, then when they start out they will lose interest quicker if they aren't having fun.

And if they are swinging and missing over and over, they will not be having fun.

No matter how much we, as parents, love the game, we will see our children leave baseball for other interests.

The intent of this book is to teach parents, so that their children will make more contact with the baseball, have fun and stay with the game longer.

CHAPTER 5
The Problem

HITTING IS HARD

The problem we have is that most kids don't know how to instinctively hit a thrown baseball. Nor should they.

And parents, as well as many coaches don't know how to teach the kids how to hit.

The result is that failure after failure in trying to hit a baseball is causing kids to switch to other sports that aren't as focused on the individual, as baseball is.

The other sports can be played from a team perspective without having a harsh light shone on individual achievement. Other sports like soccer or lacrosse allow kids to participate but also allows them to blend in. They can be a small piece in a larger mosaic.

BASEBALL DOESN'T ALLOW THAT

In baseball you are given a bat and an opportunity 3-4 times a game to be in the spotlight, where all eyes are on you and whether you fail or succeed is evident to all.

In baseball, the game stops and asks you to perform, all by yourself, several times a game...with what seems like the whole world watching. And if you continue to swing and miss it isn't fun.

After all, the longest and most embarrassing walk in sports is that 60-foot, slow walk back to the dugout with your bat, after striking out again and having your Dad, Mom, Grandparents, friends, girlfriends etc. silently watching you.

"Get em next time Joey" rings hollow when you have heard it too many times.

If you do this too often, you will leave the game. Who wants to feel embarrassed or even ridiculed over and over?

It is pretty daunting to a child. So daunting that if you fail enough it will drive you to leave the sport of baseball for safer environs way before you need to.

I don't want children to be forced due to embarrassment, to have to choose another sport.

Because once a child "switches" to another sport, or none at all...They don't come back.

I want to solve this problem for many children...and parents.

LET'S START WITH THE PARENTS

Many parents give of their time and take their child out to throw Batting Practice (BP) to them in an effort to teach them to hit.

Throwing Batting Practice to your child is "not" teaching your child. Often you are just throwing to him and hoping he hits it.

This is admirable and even a bonding experience with your child. But without proper instruction it will not be successful.

For many when you first take your child to the park or backyard for some batting practice it might go something like this. "Here Joey, I am going to pitch the ball to you."

You say things like:

- Here you go. Hit it!
- Keep your eye on the ball!
- Don't swing so hard.
- Swing harder

- Swing like you mean it!

- Slow down...speed up

Often the child will swing and miss over and over, and you will get frustrated and it will not be a good day at the park.

Your words of advice that start out as encouragement, may change to words of frustration and anger. Your cheerful comment of "keep your eye on the ball", may change to "how many times do I have to tell you to keep your eye on the ball!"

Your disappointment will shine through and may actually start to sound to your child like "pick up your socks, how many times do I have to tell you to pick up your socks!"

On the rare occasion he hits it, he won't know why or how to replicate that swing.

Your child will get discouraged and even mad at you...the whole baseball experience will be a negative one. And you may walk away saying my child just isn't cut out for baseball.

Well, you may be wrong...dead wrong. He just wasn't taught how to do it.

Sometimes, even parents who were good hitters and played at high levels have a difficult time teaching their own children to hit.

For a lot of parents who enjoyed success due to hard work but also had natural talents, have a difficult time translating how they just "did it", to a method their child understands.

It can cause a lot of frustration with the parent. They can't understand why the child just doesn't get what came so naturally to them.

This frustration and tension between the parent and the child can become the root cause the child loses interest early in baseball. The parent is working hard to help his child, but the child senses the disappointment of his parent. A child doesn't want to disappoint or be embarrassed so they may rebel.

It is like trying to teach your own child how to drive a car. Have you ever experienced that either as a parent or as the child?

What comes so naturally to you after years of driving experience, can be mind-boggling when your child doesn't have the instincts right away. Tensions rise quickly. We don't have instructions to offer our child, for the reactions and decisions we make from our years of experience.

Or, your child may even look pretty good hitting the soft tosses you are throwing to him, but when they enter a game and things speed up, they may not have the same success at hitting the ball as they did when you were tossing it in at 50-60% of the speed in the game.

The form he was using against your slower speed may not work when the pitches travel faster.

This gradual failure may occur any time a child moves up a rung or to an older level. What worked for him at a lower level may not continue to work as the game speeds up and the talent level improves.

What will you do if your child can't seem to hit a baseball when he is starting out? Or when he moves up the ladder and he begins to experience failure?

How do you fix the dreaded but unexplained, swing and miss?

What will you do when you don't know how to help your child? You will probably continue to give of your time and throw more and more BP to them. Once again, this will not help if they continue to use a form that won't succeed. It will reinforce failure.

COACHES

When you realize you can't help your child you may relinquish him or her to the Little League coach or the Babe Ruth coach? What if the Little League coach is the local accountant in town, a good guy who is coaching the Little League team because he has the time but has very little knowledge of the game?

Or maybe the Babe Ruth coach is the local pharmacist with a son on the team, or even the JV coach who is the 7th grade music teacher and took the job with good intentions, but really, he only needed the extra money?

Well your child may not find the help he needs to be successful, have fun or stay with the game. Nobody continues to do something they are not good at, get frustrated at or are embarrassed doing.

Many coaches at Pee Wee or Little League levels when they first assemble the kids on their team will give each kid a chance to grab a bat and take batting practice.

Depending on how well each kid does, the coach assesses their ability and assigns, at least mentally, who his good players are going to be. The kids get classified and put into groups that have a pecking order based on perceived talent. The kids quickly pick up on this. Children, as well as many adults, derive their own self-worth based on others' opinions of them.

This "classification" can be the beginning of a kid's withdrawal from baseball. If he is "told" he is not good, he begins to feel he is not good. Nobody likes to feel they are inferior to others in any endeavor.

I have personally seen many young kids leave baseball, due to early failure, yet go on to be very good athletes and perform well in other sports. Had they stayed with the game, in time, with growth and maturity may have become a very good baseball player. But we will never know because the inability to make contact drove them away.

Conversely, I have seen many children who mature quicker and are bigger at a younger age who have early success in Little League, yet eventually leave the game also when they move up to the next levels. The success they enjoyed early was due to natural athletic ability and being bigger than the competition, not necessarily because they had a correct "approach" to hitting.

When the game speeds up, any flaws in their hitting style show up and they begin to feel the same frustrations as the child just starting out. Without proper instruction they will leave the game for the same reasons as the newcomer.

People will often say, "I don't know what happened to him, he used to be so good".

Nothing happened to him. The game changed, and he didn't. The game sped up.

These same kids, if taught to make contact, would also stay with the game longer.

It is not the coaches' fault who are giving of their time. Without them what would we do? They do the best they can, but if they don't understand how to teach hitting, and most people don't, many children face potential failure.

The only encouragement or instruction often are things like "keep your eye on the ball, son", or "get closer to the plate".

Well-intentioned, and most likely enthusiastic encouragement, but it isn't teaching the kid to make contact and probably confusing the child more than anything.

And there are some parents who excelled in baseball and were wonderful hitters but even they have difficulty "teaching" how to hit a ball. Often the success a parent may have had was a result of simply being a good athlete with good hand-eye coordination.

But when asked to teach what came so naturally to him, he will have difficulty explaining step by step what is required, or what he did.

It is often noted that the star players in baseball usually don't make the best coaches. It is difficult to translate to another, skills that came naturally to them. They don't have a process to offer. They just did it.

But those that had talent, but needed to work hard, spent hours and hours to refine that talent. They developed processes and worked tirelessly on these processes, to get them to higher levels.

Now when these individuals are asked to explain to someone else what they did to be successful, they have a recall of a blueprint that worked for them and can share that, in a way that makes sense to others.

I want to share a Blueprint for success with you so that you will understand it, own it, and so that you can give it away.

HOPE

Well, as it turns out you can teach new young players how to make contact with the ball, and make contact more often, and it is not by simply devoting your time to throw more and more batting practice (BP) and offering encouragement.

Children need to be taught **HOW** to hit and **YOU** can do it.

Very few kids wake up one day and know how to hit a baseball. Most need to be taught how to do it.

Hitting is not something that everyone has an innate talent to do. Some are better than others but if children are shown the wrong technique, or worse yet shown none, more pitching to them will only reinforce the wrong way to do it. These youngsters will get discouraged assuming they can't hit, get labeled into that category and leave the game.

Your child will not stay with the game either if he is failing, just to please you, the parent. And if they do, they will resent you for it.

So you need to teach them. That's right...you!

Even if you never played the game or were not very good at it, you can teach them to hit. And I will show you how!

Youngsters may face the same dilemma of swinging and missing with no explanation at various points in their baseball journey, even after having had some success at lower levels...and the solution will be the same.

CHAPTER 6

Success for a Child.
What Does it Look Like?

For us as adults, how we view success for our children may be quite different than what a child just starting out in baseball views as success.

Success early for a child isn't always about hitting .300 or a home run. Sometimes it is simply putting the ball in play, being in the flow of the game.

Success can be hitting a ground ball or a lazy fly. It can be just simple contact and the ability to "run it out" and trot off the field feeling victorious because they put the ball in play.

Making out by putting the ball in play feels totally different than swinging and missing to a young child starting out. A strikeout or a ground out are the same in the box score and although neither adds to your average, don't tell that to a child.

That feeling of being in the flow of the game can be enough for him/her to feel a part of the action. To be part of the team.

Or maybe he makes contact and gets on base because of an error. He is on the base-paths, and maybe he even gets his uniform dirty. He comes back to the bench and gets high fives. Smiles abound.

He gets an opportunity to tell others in the dugout what happened "out there". Later on, or tomorrow in school he can join in the conversation about the game, because he was involved in it.

He is proud, he is happy, he belongs, he is one of the guys.

This is what success feels like to a youngster in the beginning. We have to remember what it was like when we were a child and not confuse that with adult views.

This elusive feeling is essential for a child to want to keep coming back to enjoy the game until he can grow some more, get stronger, or just give him some time to figure out how to get better.

Do you remember as a youngster, playing a game and getting your uniform dirty? And then wanting to keep that uniform on as long as possible. Not wanting to take it off?

The dirt on your uniform was a badge of honor. A symbol to anyone walking by that you were just part of something bigger, you were involved with a group of teammates in something important on the baseball field, the diamond...the Big Stage!

We can't confuse our view of success with that of a kid just starting out and looking to fit in. Maybe we have to admit that we don't like our kid making an out because it might make us look bad. That maybe our ego is in the way.

The luckiest kid out there on the field is the one who is having fun, playing a game. His view of success may be a lot different than ours unless we poison him with a wrong version of success.

Making contact, running it out, getting dirty, talking with the guys later about being on the bases, feeling as "one of the guys"...this might be what makes your child happy. He may not be the best one out there, but he might be the happiest.

This kid will want to come back tomorrow!

Let's talk about how to make this happen...

CHAPTER 7
Making Contact

For kids starting out, making contact should be the primary concern. **And having your bat on the same plane as the plane the ball travels on, for a longer period of time will increase the chances of making contact.**

This is simple right? But true.

The concept behind this philosophy is called **Contact Hitting.**

*In this photo of a Texas Ranger, you see him making contact and putting the ball in play. His bat is level, has been on the same path of the ball throughout his swing, and his **Top Hand** has orchestrated the entire swing start to finish. Always remaining on top. ©ZUMA Press/ ZUMA Press*

It is no secret that the more often you make contact with the ball the better chance you have of getting a hit, the higher your average will be and the more fun you will have no matter what level you are playing at.

But remember, for now we are dealing with newcomers and making contact is essential to their staying with the game.

As we discuss how to do this we will be assuming that we are dealing only with fastballs. As kids start out they will see primarily only fastballs in the first couple of years, eventually graduating to curveballs, etc. But if someone cannot master how to hit a fastball, they will have no chance at curveballs or when pitches start changing speeds, etc.

So, let's consider that a fastball, or straight ball, travels from the pitcher to the batter on one plane...a straight line if you will.

I think we would all agree that if the ball is coming in on one straight line, the best chance to make contact would be to have your bat travel on that same line for as long a period as possible.

Or to put it another way, to have your swing get on that line as quickly as possible and remain on that line throughout your swing.

TOP HAND HITTING

ILLUSTRATION # 1

- Barrel of Bat and ball on the same line
- Multiple points of contact

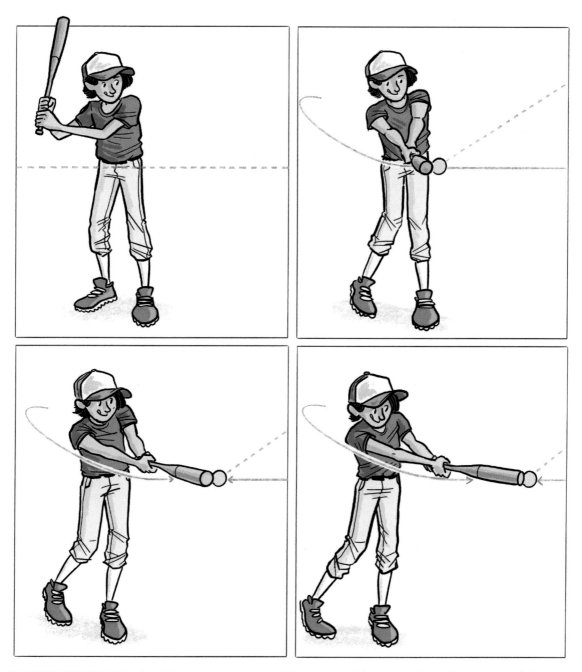

ILLUSTRATION # 1 - *In this sequence you will see that Riley Dude has the Barrel of the Bat and the pitched ball on the same "line" early in the swing and throughout the swing, creating multiple points of contact.* **Top Hand** *is on top and controlling the swing.*

By doing this you create multiple possible points of contact between the ball and the bat.

As a right-hander you could hit the ball late and to right field, or early and to left or hit it up the middle. You could pop it up or hit a weak grounder. You could also hit it foul...which for a kid starting out, sometimes that is a moral victory until success comes. And...you could also hit a line drive base hit.

But let's not forget what we said about what success looks like to a kid just starting out. We are trying to make contact and put the ball in play. This is going to make the game fun and make him feel like he is part of the game, in the flow...make him want to come back tomorrow. We will work on refining the swing and change what success looks like later.

But for now, we want to hit the ball. Make contact. Run it out.

We will discuss how to do this shortly.

CHAPTER 8

Today's Style...
Launch Angle—The Problem

Before we discuss the "solution" we need to know what the "problem" is.

When kids are left on their own to figure out how to swing, they can develop all sorts of bad habits without even knowing it. Or if taught wrong, refine bad habits without even knowing it.

The trend today in Professional Baseball is for hitters to create a "Launch Angle", or as it used to be called, an "Uppercut", for maximum distance. Home runs and how far they travel is a fascination in the game today. Creating a launch angle is all about developing an uppercut that when bat meets ball, will cause the ball to go in the air and possibly go far.

Who wouldn't want that? But there are significant drawbacks to this approach, particularly for someone just starting out. For the occasional times a batter will hit the ball using this uppercut swing, there will be many, many more times he swings and misses.

In this photo of a Pittsburgh Pirate, his Launch Angle swing obviously didn't get back up in time to hit the ball. For a child starting out, if he is left on his own, and his bat is too heavy for him he will drop the barrel of the bat to compensate and create a Launch Angle swing without knowing it. As a parent or coach, you should watch for this! ©ZUMA Press/ZUMA Press

For parents and the Little League coach they may adopt this method to teach children because they see it on TV. But this approach is the complete opposite of what I am trying to convey here.

Consider that in Little League the ball is traveling 60–70 MPH at only 45 feet, and the batter must decide to swing or not in less than half a second and then get the bat to the point of impact.

Not much time, right?

So common sense would tell us that the best chance of getting the bat to the ball would be a straight line from the bats starting position to the impact point.

But using an uppercut is not a straight line, takes longer to reach the impact point and significantly reduces the # of points of impact that the bat can meet the ball…

Once again, consider that a fastball comes in on one plane…a straight line if you will.

With an uppercut, the bat goes down under the plane that the ball travels on and then comes back "up" to meet the ball on that plane. The problem here is that it takes longer and there is only one spot where the bat can meet the ball effectively…the intersection point…and the bat and ball must arrive at that spot at the exact same time.

LAUNCH ANGLE

ILLUSTRATION #2

- Barrel of bat and ball on different lines

- Only one point of contact

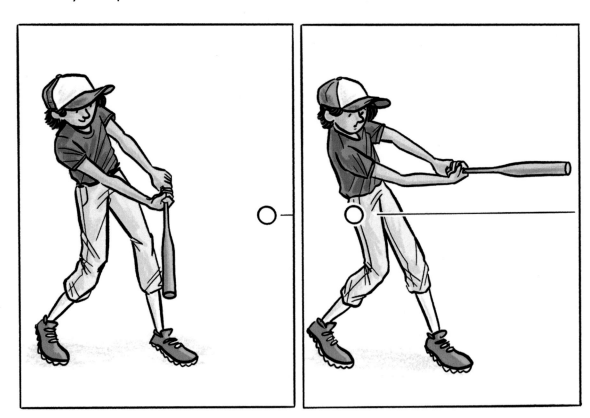

ILLUSTRATION #2 - *This sequence shows how the Launch Angle has the Barrel of the Bat traveling down under the path of the ball. It then has to come back up to only one intersection point with the line the ball is traveling on. Riley Dude doesn't get there in time and swings and misses. Focus on the path that the Barrel of the Bat takes.*

Physically what happens is that a right-handed hitter when in his batting stance has his right hand on top of the left hand on the bat. But with an uppercut or launch angle swing, when he begins his swing the top hand on the bat goes down underneath the bottom hand and then must travel back up to become the top hand again. **The problem here is that the Barrel of the Bat goes wherever your Top Hand goes.**

So, the Barrel of the bat spends almost all of its time in the swing frantically trying to get back to the plane the ball is traveling on in order to make contact.

And obviously it limits the number of impact points with the ball to only one spot. And that spot is only where the Barrel of the Bat comes back up to intersect the plane that the ball is traveling on.

LAUNCH ANGLE
ILLUSTRATION #3

- Top hand becomes bottom hand

- Barrel of bat goes where top hand goes

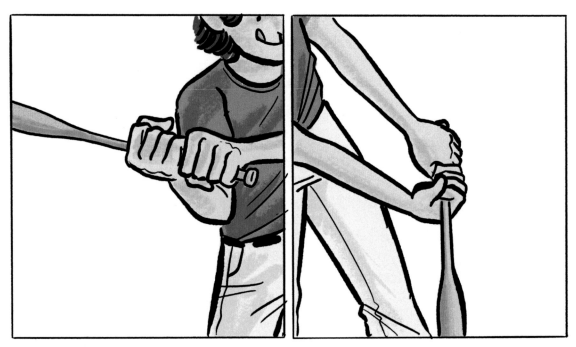

ILLUSTRATION #3 - *The focus in this sequence is on Riley Dude's Top Hand going under and becoming the bottom hand...And of course, the Barrel of Bat follows. Bat and Ball are now on different lines.*

The first wrong move is the right elbow dips in towards the waist, the right shoulder follows and dips down, the top hand goes down below the original bottom hand and then comes back up to meet the ball. The barrel of the bat follows the same path.

LAUNCH ANGLE

ILLUSTRATION #4

- First move, elbow dips in

- Second move, shoulder dips down

- Third, Top Hand and Barrel go under

- All movements are simultaneous

ILLUSTRATION #4 - *In this sequence you will see the dip movement of the elbow and shoulder and consequently Riley Dude's Top Hand and Barrel of Bat going under the line the ball. This creates the eventual "miss" of the ball by not getting there in time and swinging under the ball.*

HERE IS WHAT IT LOOKS LIKE IN REAL LIFE:

AND HERE IS WHAT IT LOOKS LIKE IN REAL-TIME IN THE MAJOR LEAGUES:

National League's San Diego Padres' Adrian Gonzalez of the San Diego Padres hits during the first round of the MLB baseball Home Run Derby in St. Louis, Monday, July 13, 2009. (AP Photo/Charlie Riedel)

*In this photo of a Launch Angle swing, notice the elbow dip in to the waist, the shoulder dip well below the other shoulder, and the **Top Hand** becoming the bottom hand and the Barrel of the Bat following the **Top Hand** ultimately bringing it well below the path of the ball.*

Take a bat and imitate the motion I just described. Experience what I am talking about.

Grab a bat. Take your stance. See that when dipping the right elbow that the shoulder follows.

Continue your swing and see that the top hand goes down below the left and then see how it needs to come back up on top to hit the ball. The barrel of the bat travels the same path.

So:

- The top hand and the barrel of the bat start out above the incoming plane of the ball,

- Travels down under the plane of the ball

- And then needs to come back up to the plane of the ball to make contact.

The problem here is that there is only one spot where the bat can meet the ball.

Let me say this again...

The bat must travel from its starting point, go down under the plane of the ball, and then back up to intersect with the plane the ball is traveling on, creating only **ONE** contact point.

LAUNCH ANGLE

ILLUSTRATION #5

- Bat in starting position

- Elbow and shoulder dip

- Top hand and barrel of bat go under

- Bat doesn't arrive on time = swing & miss

ILLUSTRATION #5 - *Here you see the correct starting point with **Top Hand** on top, but then the dip of the whole right side causing the **Top Hand** and Barrel of Bat to go under the line of the ball, then come back up late and miss the ball.*

This is why in today's Major League games you will see the catcher call for a high fastball...and even stand up when giving the target. A batter with a Launch Angle swing will rarely ever catch up to high heat from just above the belt to the letters. His bat has too far to travel. He needs to bring the barrel down under the ball path and then must get it back up to the path the ball is on and the exact single spot where the bat and ball would intersect.

Given that the ball is traveling at a high speed, and the batter must decide to swing or not within fractions of seconds, and that the bat moves at a high speed...All adds to the fact that it is very difficult to be precise and arrive at that spot exactly when the ball does.

It also forces a batter to commit to swinging way too early, before he has located the ball, just to get to that contact point before the ball does.

This is why in Major League games you see so many checked swings for strikes and so many swings and misses at the low outside curve or slider. It is maddening to viewers to watch so many Major Leaguers swing at pitches bouncing in the dirt, or checked swings being called strikes.

Because they have this Launch Angle swing which takes longer to get to a contact point, they have to start their swing earlier to catch up to a fastball... And then can't react to the "break" or hold up their swing when the pitch is a breaking ball. Make sense?

The chances of swinging and missing at fastballs are quite high also. As a matter of fact, all you have to be is "off" by a millisecond and you will not get to that spot in time.

Often this will result in the illusion that the "batter swung right through the ball", when in fact his bat traveled to that "spot" from underneath the plane of the ball, didn't get back up in time, and arrived at the "spot" just under the ball as the ball passed the "spot".

In this photo of Nick Markakis when he was with the Baltimore Orioles his Launch Angle swing actually shows the shadow of the baseball on his bat. The ball is passing over the Barrel of his bat, which is underneath the ball, and when the Barrel gets back up to the path the ball was on.... It is too late! It will appear as though "He swung right through that ball" ©ZUMA Press/ ZUMA Press

This swing, when missing the ball, will always be because the barrel of the bat, the bat head, is below the ball. And when traveling back up will arrive late at the only contact point possible.

The pitching coach mantra today in Major League baseball to get batters out is to throw "high fastballs" and "low breaking balls". They have come to understand, that even at the Pro Level, batters with a Launch Angle will have extreme difficulty hitting the high fastball (belt to letters).

This results in the high number of swings and misses and strikeouts we see on TV today.

So, if major leaguers cannot hit the high fastball, your child using the same swing will probably have difficulty also.

But remember that the illusion that he has swung through the baseball is so mesmerizing, that even parents, fans and coaches believe that he will surely hit the ball next time...after all, he looks so darn good swinging through the ball.

And also remember...It is impossible to swing through a ball.

COMPARISON OF TODAY'S STRIKEOUT LEADERS TO FORMER HOME RUN LEADERS

When batters employ a contact hitting strategy, they are not abandoning power. It is certainly possible to hit for power and also swing to make contact.

Typically contact hitters will see most of their power-hitting into the alleys in left and right, or down the lines. Singles and doubles are the major output of contact hitting, but home runs are definitely part of the equation

Contrary to popular belief, Hank Aaron and Willie Mays were contact hitters despite all the Home Runs they hit.

HANK AARON

Hank Aaron, arguably the best Home Run Hitter of all time or at the very least the second-best, never struck out more than 100 times in a season despite hitting 755 home runs. As a matter of fact, only 4 times in a season did he strike out more than 80 times.

Over 21 seasons he averaged just 66 strikeouts a season and was predominantly a top hand hitter. He generated most of this power with the strength in his forearms and his weight distribution and body torque.

WILLIE MAYS

Willie Mays hit 660 Home Runs and also averaged just 66 strikeouts a season. **In contrast, here is a list of the 2018 Strikeout Leaders and Home Runs with**

Aaron and Mays added in with their average season stats over 20 years.

AVERAGE SEASON OVER CAREER

NAME	HOMERUNS	STRIKEOUTS
H. Aaron	37	66
W. Mays	33	66

2018 SEASON STATS

NAME	HOMERUNS	STRIKEOUTS
Y. Moncada	17	217
G. Stanton	38	211
J. Gallo	40	207
C. Davis	16	192
C. Taylor	17	178
J. Upton	30	176
P. Goldschmidt	33	173
B. Harper	34	169

As you can see, today's hitters utilizing the Launch Angle approach struck out significantly more times than two of the All-Time Home Run Leaders did.

It may be safe to say that the Launch Angle allows more hitters to hit home runs but at the expense of striking out more.

Point being made is that you don't have to have a Launch Angle to hit Home Runs or hit for power, as both Aaron and Mays had a level swing approach to fastballs.

Keith Hernandez, one of my favorite players, also had a classic Top Hand level swing approach to baseball and discusses this often during his Mets broadcasts.

CHAPTER 9
There Is A Solution

Luckily...*THERE IS A SOLUTION.*

Hopefully by now, you have realized the inherent flaws and difficulty that the Launch Angle swing brings to making consistent contact with the ball.

I have a method that

- Will show how you how to make contact with the ball

- Will make sense to you.

- You can convey it to your child, so it makes sense to him

- You can then teach this method to him.

It is extremely important that you believe the method. When you believe something, you can convince someone else through your own passion and direction, that it will work for them too.

It is said in life that "whether you believe something is, or something isn't, either way you are going to be right". If you have a firm belief in this process, any process, you can teach someone and then they will often believe in you, and therefore the process.

Once you involve them in how to do it and they see the results, the will own it, and it will become theirs.

TOP HAND HITTING

My technique is called **"Top Hand Hitting"** and is designed to make contact with the ball more often. It is based on simplicity and it is based on common sense.

The basic premise of **Top Hand Hitting** is creating a level swing from start to finish.

A swing that will have your bat on the same level as the pitched ball for a longer period of time, increasing the odds that the bat will make contact with the ball...Or as we said earlier, the ball sometimes will actually make contact with the bat.

"Top Hand Hitting"— very simply this means that the **Top Hand** on the bat must always remain as the dominant hand throughout the swing. From the initial batting stance through the swing and contact with the baseball.

Getting the bat on the same plane that the ball is traveling, as soon as we can, will be our goal...and it starts with the **Top Hand**.

For you see, where the Top Hand goes, the Barrel of the Bat follows.

TOP HAND HITTING

ILLUSTRATION #6

- Ball coming in on straight line

- Top hand and barrel of the bat are on the same line as ball

- Collision course of bat and ball

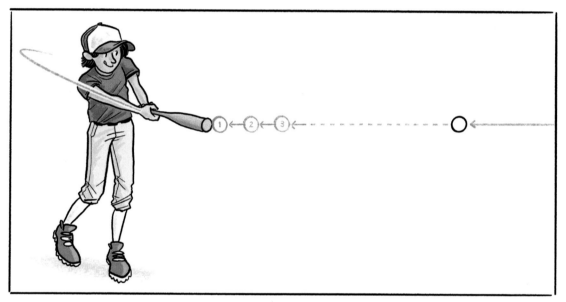

*ILLUSTRATION #6 - Riley Dude is using **Top Hand** Hitting with his **Top Hand** in control of the swing. His **Top Hand** and the Barrel of the Bat are both on the same line as the incoming ball, creating multiple points of contact. Riley Dude makes contact with the ball!*

IN CONTRAST:

LAUNCH ANGLE

ILLUSTRATION #7

- Ball coming in on straight line

- Top hand and barrel of bat are under the line of ball

- Swing and miss

***ILLUSTRATION #7** - In this swing, again, Riley Dude is going under the line of the ball and swings and misses. Notice the path of the ball...and the path of the launch swing.*

What we want to create is:

- The shortest distance to the ball and point of contact
- The quickest path,
- A level swing
- And multiple points of contact with the ball

...as opposed to just one point of contact when using an uppercut swing.

This method is SIMPLE. It is not complicated. It makes too much sense.

You can learn it.

You can teach it.

Promise.

CONSIDER THIS:

To emphasize how Contact Hitting can raise one's chances of hitting the ball and consequently enjoy more success, take a look at below.

- In the major leagues, a full season would give a player 500 At Bats over a season
- A full season is approximately 26 weeks (April through September).
- Over the course of a season if a player had:

  200 hits it would = a .400 average

  150 hits it would = a .300 average

  125 hits it would = a .250 average

  100 hits it would = a .200 average

- So, the difference between a .250 hitter and a .300 hitter is 25 hits over a 26 week season. (150 hits vs. 125 hits)

That means that a player getting just one extra hit a week would hit .300 and be a possible star as opposed to being an average hitter.

- And a .200 hitter who might not last in the big leagues could become a .250 hitter and maintain a job for a longer period of time, with just one extra hit a week.

- This same basic math applies to Little League and High School etc.

   High School - 20 games – 80 at-bats – 6 week season

   20 hits = .250

   26 hits = .325

   1 extra hit per week....

- My **Top Hand Hitting** approach would create more contact and could very possibly extend the career of not just a .200 hitter in professional ball, but could give the J.V. High School player a chance to compete at the Varsity level...Etc, etc. by creating more contact with the ball.

SO HOW DO WE DO THIS?

Well, review the Illustrations we just showed you. Understand the perils of the Launch Angle. It takes a long route to the ball by going under the line it is coming in at and has to come back up to **only one** intersection point. This creates many swings and misses.

Clearly in this picture of the Launch Angle the Barrel of the Bat had no chance to get to the One Contact point in time. ©ZUMA Press/ZUMA Press

The **Top Hand** approach gets the **Barrel of the Bat** on the same plane as the ball, as early as we can, and for as long as we can, creating many more opportunities to hit the ball.

*Once again, the **Top Hand** directs the Barrel of the Bat onto the same path the ball is traveling on early and throughout the swing. It creates multiple points of contact for the bat to hit the ball....or in some cases for the child, the ball actually hitting the bat! ©ZUMA Press/ZUMA Press*

Simple, right?

So before we start telling the child **WHAT** to do, let's tell them **WHY** first!

I believe children are smarter than we give them credit for. So, it is important to tell your child what you are trying to do.

After you read this entire book and go through the 8 Step Process both in the written word and in the video, take time to explain to your child, the path of the ball and the path of the bat...as simply as you can.

I'll bet they understand that. And if it makes sense they will be more willing to try it.

So, once again, let's look at the first Illustration that we started with.

We began with the **Top Hand Swing**, with the **Top Hand** and the **Barrel of the Bat** on the same line as the ball coming in. Show this to your child. Show them Riley Dude and how his bat and the ball are on a collision course. They will "get it".

TOP HAND HITTING

ILLUSTRATION #8

- **Top Hand** in Control
- **Top Hand** in Top
- Barrel of the Bat follows the **Top Hand**
- Barrel of the Bat on the same line as incoming ball
- Collision Course!

Illustration #8 - *This shows Riley Dude swinging the right way with the **Top Hand** in control and the Barrel of the Bat following the **Top Hand** onto the path of the pitched ball...and success!*

Contact...run it out...get dirty...feel a part of the team...fun for your child!

Once when I was trying to teach a nephew of mine how to hit, I began by having him swing and tell him to keep his top hand on top, etc...He was more interested in science and angles and video games than he was baseball at the time.

In the middle of my "teaching" him, he blurts out "but what if I hit the ball and it explodes into a million pieces like a meteor that is on a collision course to hit earth". I was like, where did that come from?

He was barely listening to me because he didn't understand what we were trying to do. But once I showed him the path of the ball and path of the bat being on the same collision course...much like a meteor crashing into earth...he got it! He understood what we were trying to do and why.

Don't underestimate your child. Sometimes coming in a door more familiar to them will make sense to them.

I can't stress enough the importance of explaining the what, and why, about what you are trying to do...

CHAPTER 10

The Five Pillars for Success

So, before we get into any drills or instruction here are some key elements that will be necessary for success and maintaining a level swing.

1. **Lightest Bat = Bat Control**

2. **Choke up**

3. **Strength**

4. **Confidence**

5. **Getting from Starting Point A to the Contact Point B**

1. LIGHTEST BAT—BAT CONTROL

It is best at first, to use the lightest bat your child can find. One that he will be able to control and have confidence in that he can get around on the ball. Later on, after playing for a while, you can switch to a little heavier bat but always use a bat that they have full control over.

If they have the wrong weight bat, one that is too heavy for them, the bat will be "swinging you". They will not have control over the bat and in order to get control of the bat, bad habits will be formed

Because the bat is too heavy, your child's first reaction when swinging will be to drop the barrel of the bat down. He will feel that he has more control over the bat this way.

To do this he will drop the elbow, shoulder and top hand simultaneously. The **Top Hand** will become the bottom hand and this will give the hitter back some strength over the bat.

This will create the **Top Hand** to become the bottom hand and will bring the bat under the plane of the traveling pitch.

We described this earlier and too heavy a bat will force your child to do this.

They unknowingly are creating an uppercut swing...Much like the Launch Angle we described earlier.

Can you understand this...Can you visualize this?

Whenever a bat is too heavy for your child, you will see them dropping the barrel of the bat down to gain more control. This is a sign, right away, that your child or any child is using a bat too heavy for them. Change to a lighter bat right away!

The **Top Hand** must always remain the top hand throughout the swing!

A light bat will allow the hitter to feel he can control the bat with his top hand.

So in the beginning, it is essential that the hitter uses the lightest bat he can find.

Remember, our goal here is to teach the new player to make contact with the ball, by giving them a plan that they understand and that will allow them to hit the ball and have fun with the game of baseball

2. CHOKE UP

Choking up on the bat or moving one's hands up an inch or two from the bottom of the bat will provide benefits not only when the child is starting out but can be beneficial throughout one's playing days.

The easiest and fastest way to swing a bat would be to hold it by the barrel end. This way all the weight would be in your hands, the bat would feel lighter and easier to swing. But we know we can't do this. The point is, the heaviest part of the bat is the barrel and the heavier the bat or the longer the bat, the harder it will be to swing.

You will also have less control of the bat and will take longer to get the barrel to the point of hitting the ball.

Think about swinging a rowboat oar. This is difficult. They are long, and the weight is far away from one's hands. A heavy bat or a long bat can feel the same way.

So, we suggest choking up on the bat when starting out, so the bat will be shorter and the weight of the barrel of the bat will be closer to the hands and body, thus making it feel lighter and easier to swing.

When a bat feels lighter, it will be easier to control, allowing the child to direct where they want the barrel to be (level) and they will be able to have a quicker swing, which will allow them to get on to the plane of the ball quicker and longer.

One could also try using a shorter bat as well, which will be lighter and will provide the same increase in control of the bat and quickness to the ball.

But I would suggest finding the longest bat but lightest bat.

The point of choking up is to increase the likelihood of making contact. Some power will be compromised, but we are trying to teach how to make contact here.

Major league hitters who are contact hitters choke up as well. Joey Votto is a great player and he chokes up...and he has averaged over 25 home runs a year over his career.

Jeff McNeill of the Mets who finished fourth in Batting Average for the National League chokes up...Many contact hitters do. Jeff hit 23 home runs in 2019.

Heck, Barry Bonds one of the best hitters of all time choked up his entire career.

 Mike Schmidt of the Phillies, Hall of Famer with 548 Home Runs always choked up situationally when he felt he needed to make contact, because it made his swing quicker and gave him more control.

So as mentioned earlier, power is not completely sacrificed when using a contact hitting style.

3. STRENGTH

Using a light bat and choking up is a great start. Next, it will be essential that the young hitter has some strength in his arms to continue to be able to "control" the bat. I am not suggesting weight lifting in any way, nor am I suggesting working on the biceps or chest. Simply put, strength and quickness in hitting are generated from the forearms and wrists.

So, a simple exercise of squeezing spring resisted hand exercisers various times through the day, or rubber balls etc., will build the muscles in the forearms, which are responsible for strength, speed and control over the bat...**it is not your biceps.**

Swinging the bat as a means of exercise will also develop the strength needed to control the bat...and is actually the most effective tool.

Strength is essential in establishing the **Top Hand** as the dominant hand.

But until the child can develop the strength needed, it is compulsory to be using the lightest bat you can find, so the child can control it.

4. CONFIDENCE

Swinging without confidence will result in a hitter swinging too soon and swinging before they have sufficiently located the ball. They will be afraid that the pitcher will throw the ball by them, and start swinging way too early.

So how does one get confidence? Well, they will need to feel comfortable that they can get around on the ball. If one worries about not being able to get around on the ball they will swing at the pitchers' motion and may not even be seeing the ball.

Swinging and hoping.

Gaining Strength as mentioned above will give the child this confidence.

As a youngster, they can feel intimidated and start their swing too soon worrying about the pitcher throwing the ball by them, but if they are using a light bat, one they feel they are in control of, they will know that they don't have to swing at the pitchers motion but can locate the ball first.

Next if they feel strong in their forearms, they will feel in command of the bat. It will feel like an extension of their arms.

These three things,

- A light bat

- Choking up

- Having strength in one's forearms giving you control of the bat

...will provide the confidence that will allow the child to have patience and wait a little longer because they will have quickness in their swing.

If they have such **mental and physical** control over the bat, knowing they have strength in their arms to be quick, then they can wait longer to swing.

This will allow the child to keep the bat in the starting position longer and not have it drift up with them as they stride forward.

The goal here is to get to a point with confidence and physical quickness that when one actually takes a pitch and doesn't swing, the bat doesn't move. It remains in the starting position. (Point A)

5. STARTING POINT TO CONTACT POINT

So we have a light bat, we are choking up, strength in the forearms, confidence that we can get around on a ball and patience to not swing too soon.

Now it is time to talk about getting from the Starting Point to making contact.

Point A is the starting point of where one holds the bat and Point B is the optimum spot where we would like to hit the ball. This would be the spot where the ball would be hit most directly, at the most level angle and with the most force.

Fortunately, the process we are discussing will provide us with multiple contact points (B, C, D, E...) increasing the odds your child will hit the ball.

By having the first 4 Pillars in place, it is at this point that we want to get from Point A to the Contact Point as quickly as we can. And the shortest distance that will allow for the quickest journey is...You guessed it...a straight line.

We will start out with a few basic drills that will reinforce the technique we are teaching. Repetition will make this technique familiar and will become your child's natural method of swinging.

We will address the stance we will use shortly.

CHAPTER 11

Wait! Learn the Process. Explain to the Child.

EXPLAIN TO YOUR CHILD WHAT YOU ARE DOING!

After you have read the **8 Step Process** below and watched the Instructional Video and you feel comfortable enough to begin teaching your child, I urge you to begin by explaining to your child exactly what you are about to tell him/her and why.

Don't rush in to begin telling him/her **what** to do.

Explain the idea of getting the bat on the same line as the ball coming in. Explain how this will increase the likelihood of him hitting the baseball...creating multiple points that the bat can hit the ball.

Tell them you are going to use a process that will show them how to do this.

It is essential that the child understands **WHY** we are asking him to approach hitting this way. If he doesn't understand why, he may argue. My way is better he may say...

Don't underestimate your child's intellect. If something makes sense to him, he will be more willing to try something. A simple explanation of the path of the ball and getting your bat on the same path for your whole swing, will create more opportunities for him to make contact.

Use examples of Major League players he likes or may know that have a similar approach. They may be in the minority, but they are out there and are successful.

Also use an example that he may understand, like my nephew and the meteor colliding with Earth. What other interest does he have that you could use to explain this concept?

If he understands this, agrees with it, and buys into it, it will become "his". He will be more apt to follow the direction.

Tell him you want to do a few drills with him before we start hitting. **Drills like the Major Leaguers do.**

Below is a Step by Step Process to follow that will allow your child to understand what you want him to do and how to do it.

There are 8 Steps...And I suggest you follow all 8 in the beginning.

As your child begins to understand and accept the approach you are teaching him, several of these steps can be eliminated later when practicing. (Steps 1, 3, 4 and 5).

You can focus only on Steps 6, 7, and 8. These are the steps many Major Leaguers do before each game.

If however, your child starts out doing well and then slips into bad habits and begins swinging and missing again, this process should be reinforced again using Steps 1-8.

This is a blueprint to teach how to make contact initially but is also a fall back blueprint for when the child goes into a slump later on. Whether it is because of bad habits or if the child moves up in age and the game speeds up some.

You can always have this process and go back to it at any time, and at any point in their playing career.

CHAPTER 12

The 8 Step Top Hand Hitting Process

INTRODUCTION TO STEPS

Following is an **8 Step Process** that will guide you on how to introduce the **Top Hand Hitting** concept to your child that will allow him to make contact with the ball.

These steps are designed to show YOU how to instruct your child. We are not teaching your child here. We are teaching you, so you can understand the process and own it.

It doesn't matter if you are a Dad or a Mom, if it is baseball or softball, or if your child is a boy or a girl. It is all the same. It is about a bat...and a ball.

The main emphasis will be to establish the **Top Hand** as the dominant hand in the swing.

We will begin with drills that don't involve a bat or a ball, but which are designed to establish a connection between the brain and the **Top Hand**.

We will continue through the process building on this connection of brain and **Top Hand** until we bring you through all 8 steps and you are throwing batting practice to your child...And he is actually hitting the ball!

Remember, what we want is your child to have fun. To hit the ball, run it out, get dirty and say to you..."Dad, Mom...that was fun, can we come back tomorrow!?"

So please read through these steps and understand them, and why we are doing them. You will need to be able to convey to your child before each step what we are about to do...and why.

Make it clear and make it simple.

If you get this process down you are paving the way for your child to engage in the great game of baseball for years to come. He will enjoy camaraderie with teammates, understand competition, learn to get along with others and handle pressure situations.

And they will learn how to win and lose with class and respect...one of life's most valuable lessons. All from the ball field.

And you will have built a situation where you can enjoy the special bonds you and your child will create together by going to their games, cheering them on, congratulating or consoling them and painting vivid memories that you will treasure for years to come.

But it all starts with your child making contact first!

So, it is our responsibility to **"Teach Your Kid to Hit...So They Don't Quit!"**

And don't forget, if you are reading this in paperback, these 8 Steps are on my YouTube channel for viewing to help you visualize what we speak about and understand it better.

In order to reach those videos, I have provided the links below that you can access by:

- **Paper Back**—type links into the browser on your computer.

- **eBook**—links are ready to click for each step in the eBook and you will be brought right to the individual Step Video.

Teach Your Kid To Hit
YOUTUBE CHANNEL

I strongly urge everyone going to the videos to
start with the introduction video...

<u>IT'S VERY IMPORTANT THAT YOU START THERE!</u>

THE 8 STEPS TO TOP HAND HITTING

At the end of each step is the video link for that particular step.

INTRODUCTION VIDEO

https://youtu.be/Lr8pgxtigt8

1. CHOPPING A TREE

Explain to him what you want him to do and why!

TELL CHILD

- What we are about to do is use a bat handle or a stick as if it were an ax and we are going to ask the child to begin to chop down the imaginary tree. You can hold a rope or something else if you want, or just an imaginary tree.

- We will ask only three things of the child.

    1. To chop that tree using his **Top Hand** as the strong hand when chopping. Concentrate on the **Top Hand**. The **Top Hand** chops a tree...not the bottom one.

    2. To make sure he is chopping at a 45-degree angle coming down, as you would if you were actually chopping at a tree.

    3. When he finishes each chop to be looking at the tree when done.

ACTIONS

- Get an old bat and saw off the handle down to 12 inches or so.

- With no stride–and with no emphasis on a batting stance or positioning, have your child swing that handle as if it was an ax and he was trying to chop down a tree. Tell him to visualize the tree **and watch the ax chop into the tree.** Make it fun!

- Make sure he is chopping down at the tree using his **Top Hand** as the forceful hand. The path of the "ax handle" should be about 45 degrees going down or more.

- Have fun with this chopping the tree.

- Don't give any direction on stance or positioning...let him have fun chopping the imaginary tree down.

- After 5-7 chops, stop and remind him to concentrate on using the **Top Hand...and to be watching the tree when done**. Then have him do five more.

- We are beginning to establish **Top Hand Dominance** through a connection between the brain and the **Top Hand** which we will continue to emphasize throughout all of these steps.

<u>SUMMARY</u>

- **Top Hand** strong

- Chop down with **Top Hand**

- Finish with gaze at the contact point

WATCH STEP ONE HERE

https://youtu.be/QVs_9GgVrxA

2. POSITIONING STANCE

Explain to him what you want him to do and why!

TELL CHILD

- What we are about to do is positioning a batting stance that he will use to chop the tree again.

- We will use this stance from now on, up and until we start hitting the ball.

- He will chop the tree the same way only using the stance.

- Just as before concentrate on using the **Top Hand** to chop that tree.

- He will finish the chop/swing with his eyes and head focused on the spot where he would have made contact with the tree.

ACTIONS

- Start to position his batting stance.

- Still using the bat handle.

- Stance – feet comfortably apart, shoulder width or a little more...maybe a little bounce in his knees.

- Arms extended back.

- Left shoulder just in front of and almost or slightly touching chin.

- The **Top Hand** on bat at nose level or slightly higher.

- Right elbow **"cocked"** (see illustration and video) facing almost directly behind him towards where the catcher would be...elbow not pointing towards the ground but almost directly "behind" him.

- This creates the right forearm to be almost parallel with the ground.

- **This posture will activate the Top Hand to be "locked-in" and in full control...think strong with Top Hand.**

- Bat handle should be pointing upwards behind him at about 70 degrees (midway between 45 and 90 degrees).

- Chop that same tree.

- After each swing/chop...stop...reset stance...proceed. Don't rush.

- Take 7-10 chop/swings and finish each with his gaze on the "contact point".

<u>SUMMARY</u>

- Stance

- Cock elbow

- **Top Hand** strong

- Chop with **Top Hand**

- Finish with gaze at the contact point

- Reset stance after each chop/swing

WATCH STEP TWO HERE ↓

https://youtu.be/3MTPywYcgj4

3. USING BAT HANDLE - SOFT TOSS

Explain to him what you want him to do and why!

TELL CHILD

- You are going to go in front of him and toss a ball to him .

- He is going to use the same stance with the bat handle that we just showed him.

- He is going to think **Top Hand** strong.

- When you toss the ball to him, he will chop/swing at the ball using the **Top Hand** but not expecting to hit it, because the bat is not long enough.

- He will chop/swing, miss and finish with his gaze at the spot where he would have made contact.

ACTION

- Position his stance as above.

- Still with the sawed-off bat, toss a ball underhand from in front of him (8-10 feet away) and have him use the same "ax" swing with the handle as if it was a full bat.

- Stress that he feels and thinks about his **Top Hand** being in full control.

- Cock that elbow.

- He will obviously "miss" the ball using just the handle, but you want him chopping at the ball and watching the ball as he chops at it.

- Stress that he sees exactly where the ball is as he misses it. Where contact would have been made. Head still and eyes on the potential contact point when he is done swinging.

__OPTIONAL__ to use different colored balls. Could be tennis balls or plastic balls for this exercise since we won't be hitting them.

- After the chop and miss, stress his eyes should be focused on where the ball would hit the bat. Make it a game by asking him after he swings what color the ball was...This will force him to keep his eye on the ball through contact.

- Have him take 10 chop/swings or so, **resetting the stance each time. Take your time. Do it right!**

- **Top Hand** strong, chop/swing with **Top Hand**, finish with gaze at the contact point.

SUMMARY

- Stance

- Cock elbow

- **Top Hand** strong

- Chop with **Top Hand** at the tossed ball

- Finish with gaze at where contact point would have been

- Reset stance after each chop/swing

WATCH STEP THREE HERE

https://youtu.be/Iqw_B0i6RuQ

4. INTRODUCE A BAT

Explain to him what you want him to do and why!

TELL CHILD

- You are going to start using a bat now...The handle is gone!

- He is going to do all the same things we have already done but now with a bat.

- Tell him we are close to begin hitting the ball.

- Tell him we are going to ask him to stride as he swings now ...if he hasn't been up to now.

- Tell him to think **Top Hand** strong...**Top Hand** in full control.

ACTION

- Position his stance as above.

- Get the lightest bat you can find.

- Choke up on the bat an inch or so.

- Stress that he feels and thinks about his **Top Hand** being in full control.

- Cock that elbow.

- Stride towards the pitcher and take several swings...chopping at a tree...45-degree angle down.

- Don't worry that the "swing" will look very much like a downward swing and not a level swing at this point. It is beginning to level off and will be level at the end.

<u>SUMMARY</u>

- Using the lightest bat and choking up

- Stance

- Cock elbow

- **Top Hand** strong

- Stride and chop with **Top Hand** at the tree

- Finish with gaze at where contact point would have been

- **Reset stance** after each chop/swing

WATCH STEP FOUR HERE

https://youtu.be/NxGDYFfcSJs

5. USE A BATTING TEE WITHOUT A BALL

Explain to him what you want him to do and why!

TELL CHILD:

- You are going to use a tee.

- You will ask him to use the same process we have been following.

- We will not use a ball but he will chop/swing at the empty spot on the tee as the contact point (that is where the tree is).

- Tell him the next 3 steps he will be hitting the ball...so concentrate.

- **Top Hand** strong.

- Swing down with **Top Hand** at empty top of tee.

- Finish with gaze at top of the tee.

ACTION

- Move to an outdoor backstop behind home plate.

- Set up a tee in the backstop around home plate facing into the fence – away from the field. Don't use a ball yet.

- Position his stance as above.

- Using the lightest bat he can find...choke up.

- Stress that he feels and thinks about his **Top Hand** being in full control.

- Stride forward and have him take several chop swings at the tee where the ball would be. (Chopping the tree).

- Make sure he knows that when he is finished swinging his eyes should be on the tee where the ball would be placed.

- Don't worry if he knocks the tee over. Pick it up. No problem. Have fun.

- Let him know the next step will be with a ball so concentrate.

<u>SUMMARY</u>

- Stance

- Focus on top of the tee

- Cock elbow

- **Top Hand** strong

- Chop with **Top Hand** at the empty tee

- Finish with gaze at the tee where the contact point would be

- Take 7-10 swings

- **Reset stance** after each chop/swing

WATCH STEP FIVE HERE

https://youtu.be/F29UExacBVM

6. USE A BATTING TEE WITH A BALL

Explain to him what you want him to do and why!

TELL CHILD

- You are going to place a ball on the tee and he is going to hit it.

- These are drills the major leaguers use.

- He needs to do the same things we have done now for the 5 previous steps.

- He will think **Top Hand** strong and swing at the ball on tee with **Top Hand**.

- He should try and hit the ball directly into the backstop.

- Tell him not to look up to see where the ball goes...it isn't going anywhere... you are in a cage.

- Tell him his focus should remain on the top of the tee where the ball was when he is done...just like he has been doing.

ACTION

- Now place a ball on the tee.

- Position stance.

- Cock elbow and activate **Top Hand**. **Top Hand** strong.

- And swing at the ball with the same stride and chop motion, trying to hit the ball directly straight ahead into the backstop.

- Stress that he feels and thinks about his **Top Hand** being in full control.

- Ensure he is watching the bat hit the ball, even after he hits it. His gaze after hitting the ball should be at the contact point (empty tee) not following the batted ball.

- When chopping a tree the front shoulder wouldn't fly open but stay compact moving towards the tree...same when he is swinging at the ball.

- Make sure that the **Top Hand is the strong and dominant hand...chopping down.**

OPTIONAL. Every third time have him stride but don't swing. Emphasize that the bat stays in the same exact starting spot as when he started his stride*

*We want hands and swing to go from Point A (Starting Point) to Point B (Contact Point) in one motion and on a straight line. There will be additional benefits down the road as he advances in levels.

SUMMARY

- Place ball on the tee

- Advise him he may want to look at where the ball goes after he hits it. **Tell him (nicely) not to**

- Position stance

- Focus on the ball on top of the tee

- Cock elbow

- **Top Hand** strong

- Swing with **Top Hand** at the ball on the tee

- Finish with gaze at where the ball was on of top of the tee

- Take 7-10 swings

- Reset stance after each chop/swing

WATCH STEP SIX HERE ↓

https://youtu.be/cz3jA2FnPes

7. SOFT TOSS HITTING INTO BACKSTOP

Explain to him what you want him to do and why!

TELL CHILD

- You are going to toss him balls and he is going to hit them into the backstop.

- Next step we will hit out into the field.

- These are drills the Major Leaguers use.

- He needs to follow everything we have been doing for 6 Steps now.

- You will toss them form the side and he will hit into the backstop.

- To watch the bat hit the ball.

- He will want to look at where the ball goes...but he must finish with his focus on where he made contact with the ball.

ACTION

- Staying in a cage behind home plate on a field remove the tee.

- Position yourself facing him about 45 degrees to his right.

- Ensure he has the correct stance and hand positioning.

- Get a bucket of balls. Using the lightest bat, and choking up, toss the ball **underhand** and on a line to him from about 8-10 feet away.

- Stress that he feels and thinks about his **Top Hand** being in full control.

- Have him chop at the moving ball intending to see it hit the bat and to hit the ball straight ahead into the cage (or right back up the middle, where the pitcher would be)...front shoulder driving towards the "tree" or the pitcher.

- His gaze after contact should be where the bat hit the ball, not following the batted ball.

- **You should notice that even though he may feel at this point that he is swinging completely down, the bat swing will be more or less level.**

OPTIONAL. Every third or fourth toss tell him to 'take" the pitch and tell him his hands should not move from their starting point.

<u>SUMMARY</u>

- Stance

- Watch the ball you are going to throw

- Cock elbow

- **Top Hand** strong

- Chop with **Top Hand** at the tossed ball

- Watch the bat hit the ball

- Finish with gaze at where the contact point of the ball was

- Take 7-10 swings

- **Reset stance** after each chop/swing

WATCH STEP SEVEN HERE ↓

https://youtu.be/S6j1Tqjl9DA

8. PITCH FROM IN FRONT OF PITCHER'S MOUND

Explain to him what you want him to do and why!

TELL CHILD

- You are going to pitch to him from the field.

- These are drills the Major Leaguers do.

- You want him to do exactly as we have been preparing in the first 7 steps.

- To swing at the ball with the **Top Hand** just as we have been doing.

- Remind him he may want to look and see where the ball goes, but he needs to see the bat hit the ball and finish with his head and eyes watching the contact point...He can look up a split second later.

ACTION

1. With a bag of balls go onto the field and prepare to pitch to the batter from in front of the pitcher's mound, about halfway between the mound and home plate.

2. The child is still using the lightest bat and choking up.

3. Use correct stance.

4. Stress that he feels and thinks about his **Top Hand** being in full control.

5. Pitch on a level plane to the child...**start with a few underhand before going to overhand.** Have him make contact, see it works, build confidence.

6. Encourage him to stride toward you, with strong **Top Hand** chop or swing at the ball trying to hit right back at you or up the middle.

7. When hitting a ball up the middle it will keep the front shoulder from "flying open".

8. Make sure he watches the bat hit the ball.

9. Make sure he is still using that strong **Top Hand** to control his swing...chopping at ball.

10. If he has trouble making contact...move closer until he begins hitting the ball and gradually move back again.

11. Eventually get yourself to the mound and the proper distance. Maybe not in the first session. You want him to make contact and feel good about himself and the game. You want to leave on the note of having your child wanting to come back. Sometimes pitching from the mound too soon can cause swings and misses...And you will have "undone" all the good to that point. Move to the mound next time.

12. **Always, always leave on a line drive...In other words, after good contact, feeling good and wanting to come back.**

13. You want him to remember that sweet feeling of making solid contact with the ball. It is a beautiful feeling. You want him to know it.

14. Maybe have him run a couple of hits out...Go to second...slide...get dirty... High five him!

15. You want to hear him say "Dad, Mom, that was fun! Can we come back tomorrow!?

<u>SUMMARY</u>

- Stance

- Focus on the ball you toss

- Cock elbow

- **Top Hand** strong

- Chop with **Top Hand** at the ball

- Level swing...Watch ball hit the bat

- Finish with gaze at where contact point was with the ball for a split second, then look

- Take 7-10 swings

- **Reset stance** after each chop/swing

- Finish on a line drive, run it out, get dirty, have fun...smile

WATCH STEP EIGHT HERE ↓

https://youtu.be/xNpMWv56-sc

Reminder. This may seem like a lot of steps and things to remember, but we are really only emphasizing the same few things over and over.

- Correct starting stance.

- Cock elbow...**Top Hand** strong.

- Stressing, both physically and mentally, the **Top Hand** being in control.

- Swinging down/level with **Top Hand** and watching bat hit the ball.

- Eyes on the contact point.

After the first few times with your child, you can begin to eliminate some of the steps, focusing mainly on Steps 2, 6, 7, 8.

Step 2 – Stance

Step 6 – Hit off the tee into the cage

Step 7 – Soft Toss from 45-degree angle

By warming up like this, it will re-establish the connection between the **Top Hand** and the Brain! Then on to Step 8.

Step 8 – BP – Batting Practice

Summary

Well, there you have it.

A process that you can understand and that you can teach to your child.

You no longer have to throw him pitches and hope he hits the ball.

You no longer have to cringe every time your child comes to bat in a game.

You no longer have to trust that someone else will teach him.

You are now the person who can teach your child to contact the baseball.

If you have read this entire book, you now understand what will not work for your child and why the "Uppercut Swing" results in swings and misses.

You will also know what to look for if your child goes into a slump. You can see if he is dropping his elbow...his shoulder. Is his **Top Hand** dropping down? You will know what to do to correct this.

You also understand the benefits of the **Top Hand** approach and the increased likelihood of your child making contact with the baseball.

You now have a philosophy and a process that you believe in and you can use to teach your child, and you can use to coach other children on Little League teams or Babe Ruth or High School.

If you use this method, you will drastically improve any child's chances of making contact...and have fun!

To recap what we discussed in this book, let me summarize.

We started with the extremely important **"STOP. READ THIS SECTION FIRST!"**

I again urge you to go back and read that if you haven't. It will layout not only what we will discuss in the book, but WHY!

It also explains how you will get the most out of the book and how to use the information best.

It will guide you to understand why it is critical to teach your child to make contact with the ball early before they lose interest.

And it will tell you the connection between the state of baseball today, how people complicate teaching the art of hitting a baseball, why parents struggle to get their kids to hit, and why kids get frustrated and quit the game.

All of which are critical for you to grasp, so you can fully believe in and own the **Top Hand Hitting** Process, and make it your own personal brand.

The stories, anecdotes and statistics will also be entertaining along the way.

And by the time you get to the 8 Step Instructional Process (written and video) at the end of the book, you will understand the approach, the reason why it will work and you will believe in it.

Next in:

- Chapter 1 we spoke about the Purpose of the Book which was to provide a method or process to the parent that he could teach to his child, which would show him how to make contact with the baseball.

- In Chapter 2, we previewed the process by providing a set of instructions to the parent that involved a Level Swing, **Top Hand** dominance and getting the barrel of the bat on the same plane as the ball for as long as we can... Which will increase the number of contact points.

- Also in Chapter 2 we stressed that although this book and this process is intended for kids just starting out, it is also applicable to anyone at any age, and it works for kids just starting out or for players who reach a point where their style is no longer working. It can revive and extend ones playing time.

- Chapter 3 showed how swinging and missing has become acceptable in baseball today...but, how that swinging and missing can disillusion a child just starting out.

- Chapter 4 shows how The State of Baseball today is creating the loss of interest by our American youth and causing them to leave Baseball for other endeavors.

- The Problem in Chapter 5 established that hitting a baseball is hard and baseball, unlike other sports, requires an individual to perform at Home Plate all by himself 4 times a game, where success or failure is immediately evident to all. Consistent failure and embarrassment will drive your child away from Baseball.

- Chapter 5 also told us that usually, neither parents nor Little League coaches know how to teach kids to hit, but with this new process YOU can do it!

- In Chapter 6 we discussed that success for kids early on is simple. Kids want to have fun while playing baseball and making contact will help them feel a part of the team and will make them want to continue.

- We discussed in Chapter 7, the obvious advantages of a level swing and creating multiple points of contact with the ball. It was here that we first introduced **Riley Dude** in Illustration form as an entertaining and visual aid for your child and as a teaching tool for the Parent.

- Chapter 8 broke down the Problem of using the Launch Angle as a method to teach kids to make contact, exposing it as the latest "fad" with the major drawback being it creates only one single point of contact between bat and ball. **Riley Dude** continued to help demonstrate the Problem visually.

- We discussed the Solution in Chapter 9. The Solution being **Top Hand Hitting**, where we create multiple points of contact by getting the Barrel of the Bat on the same line of the Ball as soon as we can, and for as long as we can. Once again, **Riley Dude** brought this to life.

  » Level Swing

  » **Top Hand Hitting**

> » The Barrel of the Bat goes where the **Top Hand** goes

> » Getting the Barrel of the Bat on the same plane as the ball

- We laid out The Five Pillars of Success in Chapter 10:

    1. Lightest Bat = Bat Control

    2. Choke up

    3. Strength

    4. Confidence

    5. Getting from the Starting Point to the Contact Point

- Chapter 11 cautions the parents to read the steps and also watch the video instructional series. BUT...to not rush out and begin teaching your child. It implores that you fully understand the Process and **THEN** explain to your child exactly what you are going to do with him, but most importantly **WHY!**

- Finally, in Chapter 12 we walked you through Steps 1-8 of the **Top Hand Hitting Process.** It laid out a physical and psychological connection between the **Top Hand** being in control and creating a level swing that drastically improves the chances of bat and ball intersecting.

The written steps **tell** you exactly how to teach your child...and the Video Steps **show** you exactly how to teach your child the **Top Hand Hitting** System.

The URL links to see the actual process on video are written in the paperback for you to copy into your browser and in the e-Book the links are provided to view immediately.

I am confident that this philosophy and process will provide you with a plan that you can use to teach your child to hit.

I recommend that you read this book slowly, and understand the concepts of **Top Hand Hitting** and a Level Swing as ways to show your child how to make contact.

Also, visit my YouTube Channel for videos of **The Introduction to the Steps** and also all **8 Individual Steps**, or find the links right in the e-Book in each step just click the link and watch.

The **8 Step Process** may seem like a lot to remember, but they are only reinforcing the same principles over and over.

As you study the principles, understand them and own them, you will have the confidence to teach them.

And you can begin to eliminate some of the Steps as your child grasps them.

(Steps 2, 6, 7, 8, will be the ones you use always going forward)

Remember, I don't want these to be my Principles. I want them to be your Principles. I want you to own them and teach them.

Good luck and have fun.

See you at the ball game!

HERE IS THE FULL VIDEO TO WATCH

https://youtu.be/zS6nm0J0wTE

About the Author

Kevin Gallagher is a person who tries on a daily basis to inspire hope in every-one he meets. This doesn't take an extreme amount of effort, but rather simply recognizing that we all struggle with something. And even if we don't know the exact worries or wounds of another, if we meet that unknown with kindness, it somehow has a soothing effect and we are all better for it.

In this book he addresses the struggle of a vast audience of parents who want to help their child participate in a sport, but lack the know-how. Kevin meets that struggle with insight and gentleness, providing hope to the parent via a solution they can learn and teach.

Kevin was a three sport athletic star in High School going on to play both College Basketball and Baseball. It was in Baseball he excelled the most.

He was a three time East Coast Athletic Conference (ECAC) All Star playing for Division 1A Pace University, University Athlete of the Year three years in a row, set six School Batting Records, was inducted into the Pace University Hall of Fame, finished in the Top Ten in batting and was an All Star playing for the Mt Vernon Generals in the Atlantic Collegiate Baseball League (ACBL) under the coaching guidance of Jack Fisher, former long-time Major League Pitcher and played with the Pittsburgh Pirates Class A team before an injury ended his career abruptly.

Kevin has also coached at numerous levels including Little League, American Legion, High School, College and in the Atlantic Collegiate Baseball League, a Major League Baseball Funded Summer League for Draft Prospects.

Writing this book was born from Kevin's own wound of having his baseball career ended prematurely, and has been a passion of his for a long, long time.

This is just another example of Kevin meeting another's struggle, in this case the parent trying to help his child, with insight, gentleness and hope.

Made in the USA
Monee, IL
31 August 2024

65005338R00079